WHO ARE YOU?
THE LIFE AND DEATH OF
KEITH MOON

JIM McCARTHY & MARC OLIVENT

CW00819881

Copyright © 2016 Omnibus Press
(A Division of Music Sales Limited)

Cover illustrated by Marc Olivent
Text by Jim McCarthy
Book illustrated by Marc Olivent

ISBN: 978.1.78305.888.4
Order No: OP56320

The Author hereby asserts his/her right to be identified as the author of this work in accord-
ance with Sections 77 to 78 of the Copyright, Designs and Patents Act 1988.

All rights reserved. No part of this book may be reproduced in any form or by any electronic
or mechanical means, including information storage or retrieval systems, without permission
in writing from the publisher, except by a reviewer who may quote brief passages.

Exclusive Distributors
Music Sales Limited,
14/15 Berners Street,
London, W1T 3LJ.

Music Sales Pty Ltd,
Australia and New Zealand
Level 4, 30-32 Carrington Street,
Sydney
NSW 2000
Australia.

Every effort has been made to trace the copyright holders of the photographs in this book
but one or two were unreachable. We would be grateful if the photographers concerned
would contact us.

Printed in the EU.

A catalogue record for this book is available from the British Library.

Visit Omnibus Press on the web at **www.omnibuspress.com**

WHO ARE YOU?
THE LIFE AND DEATH OF
KEITH MOON

JIM McCARTHY & MARC OLIVENT

OMNIBUS PRESS

London / New York / Paris / Sydney / Copenhagen / Berlin / Madrid / Tokyo

DRUMS AND DRINK AND ROCK AND ROLL

This graphic novel *Who Are You?* is based on, and adapted from, Tony Fletcher's *Dear Boy: The Life Of Keith Moon*, originally published by Omnibus Press in 1998.

I first read Tony's book around ten years ago, after my book *Voices Of Latin Rock* had been published in America. With a foreword by Carlos Santana, it was another riotous tale of sudden success followed by inter-band tensions and subsequent hard drug and alcohol use, all accompanied by a torrent of superb groundbreaking music. I soon realised that Tony's book was an intensely researched and gripping biography and was gratified when it crossed over beyond the field of rock, enjoying both critical success and healthy sales. At least three of *Dear Boy*'s major themes resonated with me strongly.

From a young age I loved drummers and drumming, and I used to play a bit myself. Keith Moon was one of many drummers who made an impact on the UK beat scene in the Sixties: among them Bev Bevan with his machine gun-like single-stroke rolls behind the original Move; Kenny Jones with his crisp beats and sinuous double-stroke rolls on recordings by The Small Faces, especially his cascading snare and toms outro to 'Tin Soldier', a mini soul masterpiece; and Bobby Elliott of The Hollies with his looser,

swinging style that enlivened his group's harmony-drenched three-minute hit singles. Later on, as my tastes developed, I saw the young and outrageously talented Richard Bailey playing with Batti Mamzelle and heard his fusion work with Jeff Beck. Meanwhile America was throwing up scores of hot drummers: Mike Shrieve of Santana, Dino Danelli from The Rascals, Bernard "Pretty" Purdie with Aretha Franklin and King Curtis, Jabo Starks and Clyde Stubblefield with James Brown's Famous Flames. The list is endless.

I studied Keith Moon's unusual and unique style and remember laughing on first hearing his dropped flam on 'Pinball Wizard' (at 1:37), in which the rhythm seems to sputter to a halt! There was always a feeling of unrestrained tension in Moon's playing. His hi-hat double sweeps throughout that particular song's verses and his tom-tom drop-ins on the outro are an aural delight. I just wish the rather dense production of The Who's *Tommy* album hadn't buried his drumming deep down in the mix as often as it did.

One other area of resonance with Tony's book was the supposition that Keith was ADHD (or ADD, essentially meaning attention hyperactivity deficit disorder). I feel that many of these acronyms denoting mental health issues, or issues within the brain's chemistry, are in their infancy and there is a long way to go before definitive treatments can be demarcated. It's interesting that Keith's drugs of choice (certainly at first) were uppers and alcohol. Both can be used, unintentionally, by ADHD sufferers to achieve some kind of brain balance, to attempt to clear the mental fog and to try to get one's life and thinking into sharper focus. They can also slow down the tumultuous mental over-activity that would result in either over-stimulated mental hyper-exertions or stultifying the sufferer into a kind of numb and procrastinating mental stasis.

Keith had many of the recognised 'traits' of an ADHD individual – the impulsive behaviour, the innate talent, which was never developed through specialised training but occurred spontaneously – and not always when required. Then there were the persistent ongoing distractions, coupled with his addictive personality and inability to stay put or stay calm for any concentrated period. He appeared to have no sense of any personal danger and was a constant risk-taker, both in his excessive use of booze and drugs and in his erratic behaviour patterns.

I was diagnosed with the symptoms of ADHD as an adult via an intensive series of tests over a one-year period and

eventually traced this behaviour all the way back to my early years. While not comparing myself to Keith Moon in any way, I certainly identified similar behaviour in myself, and such is the nature of this condition (which many people assume to be sort of 'made up') that you are unaware of it, even though you know, or can come to realise, that something is 'wrong'. Much of the time it feels like laziness or an inability to enjoy any natural life progression. Even with the aid of, say, cognitive behavioural therapy to examine thought processes and the behaviours attached, it is still hard to realise this in yourself. For many it remains undetected for a lifetime. Back in the Sixties and Seventies, when Keith's symptoms were developing apace, there was little in the way of insight into this disorder.

The third area in which I felt a great sense of identification with Keith Moon was in his addictive impulses and alcoholism, which some would say are two sides of the same complex coin. Reading and researching Tony's book for a second time for this graphic adaption and digging into the detail, I developed a growing sense of dread as I saw Keith hurtling towards his early demise at the at the age of 32.

RESOURCES

Dear Boy: The Life Of Keith Moon. Tony Fletcher (Omnibus Press, 2005 edition)

Alcoholics Anonymous UK
For persons who may have issues
around the use of alcohol.
National Helpline 0845 769 7555
www.alcoholics-anonymous.org.uk

Narcotics Anonymous UK
For people who may be experiencing
issues around the use of drugs and alcohol.
National Helpline 0300 999 1212
www.ukna.org

These self-help fellowships are available in many other countries.

He became increasingly aware that the many detoxes, admissions to rehab and stomach pumps indicated something was seriously off beam. He always picked up the first drink or drug – the one that does the damage and sets the entire mentally obsessive and physically compulsive merry-go-round off again – with increasingly severe and distressing results. Relationships suffered, his playing skills diminished, he lost his strength, and a personality that was once buoyant, infectious and light-hearted became darker and secretive as the illness progressed. He became engulfed in fears, both rational and irrational.

I recognised the fear in his face during the video for the song 'Who Are You', recorded in The Who's own studio in May 1978 when he had just over three months left to live. Here is both a little boy in a young(ish) man's body and a frightened addict gripped by the innate terrors attached to addiction and heavy destructive drinking. He is very bloated – 12 years of excess is etched into his once handsome features.

For most of us it is logical to think that if you have 'everything' in life, why can't the individual simply use their willpower and just *stop*? But addiction is more complex than that. Although at first intensely pleasurable, the user will drink alcohol for many reasons: as a form of rocket fuel (aka lunatic soup?), as an early morning booster, as a real energising pick-me-up. It can be used as a form of tranquiliser, to calm high velocity mental thought processes. It is a great leveller, allowing seemingly 'normal' social intercourse, permitting the essentially shy and often socially inept alcoholic to blend in with his fellows, for a while at least. It can help eliminate the oft described feelings of alienation and 'otherness' that is the strange bedfellow of the incipient alcoholic/addict.

Whether this is a genetically imprinted pattern or a learned behaviour or a result of accumulated family disorders and social pressures or a mixture of all of these is a moot point. What is obvious is that alcoholism wreaks havoc in every area of the sufferer's life.

Apart from ongoing daily abstinence, I have never seen a full-blown alcoholic control this malady at all and I've seen thousands over the years. I myself got into trouble quite early on through sustained drinking and drug use and ended up in a very bad place and, thank God, managed to climb out of this personal hell in my latter twenties, back in 1985.

I was also very intrigued by Keith's initial meeting with the noted drug counsellor Meg Patterson, in which she stated that Keith needed an immediate intervention from Jesus – in essence, that he needed a total spiritual healing. Reading the biography, I was unaware of any real religious influences in Keith's childhood or spiritual longings in Keith at all.

So my sense of identification with Keith Moon, in this area, is paramount, regardless of the perceived differences in his money, abilities, success or fame. I felt a great sense of sadness as I saw his life cut short, just as he was realising the serious nature of his problem.

In the modern era, almost five decades on from when The Who and Keith Moon first implanted themselves on our consciousness, the rock and pop bazaar appears to be populated with dull, bland, inoffensive characters, more suited to a job behind the counters of your local bank or supermarket than a public stage. Generally, the music scene is so square now it hurts. Keith Moon was a precocious lightning bolt from the drab environs of Alperton, Wembley in West London. He was a mini supernova that exploded and shone with a very bright intensity for those few years.

In these days of manufactured pop pap, Keith stands out like a true star. He abounded with the 'X' factor, he had 'it' in droves; that indefinable chemistry and talent that all the truly great bands or individuals have that occurs naturally without the need for insipid televised talent contests to single it out. You can't buy it, you either got it or you don't. You can try and package it (and the industry always tries to do that) but someone like Keith, with his unpredictable and total lack of regard for authority, would confound the best attempts to put him in a safe box and stifle his personal brilliance. As Keith once so aptly put it, "*If you don't like it, you can fuck off!*"

Jim McCarthy, 2016

It's hard to front big social gatherings without a defence, an ally -- a friend...?

Annette, I don't really want to go... I want to stay sober tonight.

C'mon, Keith, we can still go, darling -- can't you just stay away from the sauce for one night?

There is always someplace, somehow and someone to supply a little strengthening of resolve. In flat 12 that need will be met -- as it has been met countless times before...

The booze has washed out of his system a bit, it takes 72 hours to clean out the last drink... but it's so hard to leave it alone -- or maybe a substitute for booze would work? Just to get you through the evening, the party and the premiere...

...just this once (once again)...

Peppermint Park,
Upper Saint Martin's Lane,
Covent Garden, London,
September 6, 1978.

The premiere of the Buddy Holly
musical starring Gary Busey --
a gala party is held to honour
the opening.

It's the go-to party
of the year. The great
and the good are in
attendance... the
cream of London's
rock 'n' roll elite...

Keith could inhabit the top tables of that
closeted world with ease... and with pleasure...

Keith, ensconced in his Roller, is taking in the Central London sights on a relatively sober night out. After earlier promises, there was booze tonight and the couple of packets of cocaine have supplied the inner brilliance needed to front this social gathering...

John Otway got picked up along the way at the premiere. The actual showing of the film followed...

Keith looks really tired. I couldn't believe him when he said he's just 32 -- he looks like he's lived three lives already.

I didn't manage to stay totally straight... I had a few tonight, not too many, and I did do that coke as well...

I didn't do so badly tonight, and those pills from the doctor will help me sleep better...

Wembley is a nondescript suburban area of North West London. In this place, with its faded industrial past...

...at the Central Middlesex Hospital on Acton Lane, on August 23, 1946, another child came into this world. He squalled, he made noise as all babies do. He was named Keith John Moon...

Keith got a firm grasp on his dad Alf's hand and looked like he'd never let go...

Alfred and Kathleen Moon (or Kit, as she liked to be known) were proud parents of the beaming tot...

Keith was developing a taste for a catchy tune...

We'll meet again, don't know where, don't know when...

Music was in his blood, in his veins, even then at the age of three years old...

Keith would sit there for hours entranced, listening to Jimmy Shand, the Scottish bandleader, or Nat King Cole, another early favourite.

Keith got himself a new sister, Linda Margaret, and the family got a new address -- a newly built council property at 134 Chaplin Road, near the Harrow Road in Wembley...

Keith was well-liked at his new school, he was considered a "lovable lad"...

Aarrrrr, aarrr there, me hearties...

Even then Keith couldn't keep still, couldn't keep a straight face...

Dad Alf tried to interest Keith in that most English of pursuits -- cricket. But Keith didn't stay at it for long -- even with blandishments from his dad....

C'mon, Nobby, you could try a bit harder...

Keith got bored with chasing newts in Barham Park with his good friend Michael Morris...

Exotic visits to Herne Bay to chase cockles and whelks would sometimes contain Keith's listlessness...

... and Whitstable, with its talk of fabled oysters, would offer views of the wild sea surrounding The Isle Of Sheppey, visible from the shoreline -- especially around the front and near The Neptune, supposedly haunted by old fishermen...

School was fits and starts and lots of daydreaming... but he loved being by water...

An overactive mind is a mind rushing everywhere to no avail... trying to hang onto thoughts, concepts and ideas -- an endless torrent of mental activity...

The 11-plus school exam came a year early because of Keith's birthdate...

...and left Keith perplexed. He took it at just 10 years old. He could have done with that extra year to prepare. Looks like he was being dumped into a secondary modern next and not a grammar school.

Alperton Secondary Modern School For Boys (the "Modern" got dropped soon thereafter). It was 1957. Keith got a new nickname. His manner was getting more pronounced, more disruptive...

...concentrating was a major struggle -- a struggle that seemed to be a lost cause...

There goes Sputnik, creating noise and attention seeking as usual...

YING TONG IDDLE I PO !

The Goons were a madcap soundtrack for a strait-laced Britain and Keith was enamoured of them like so many others...

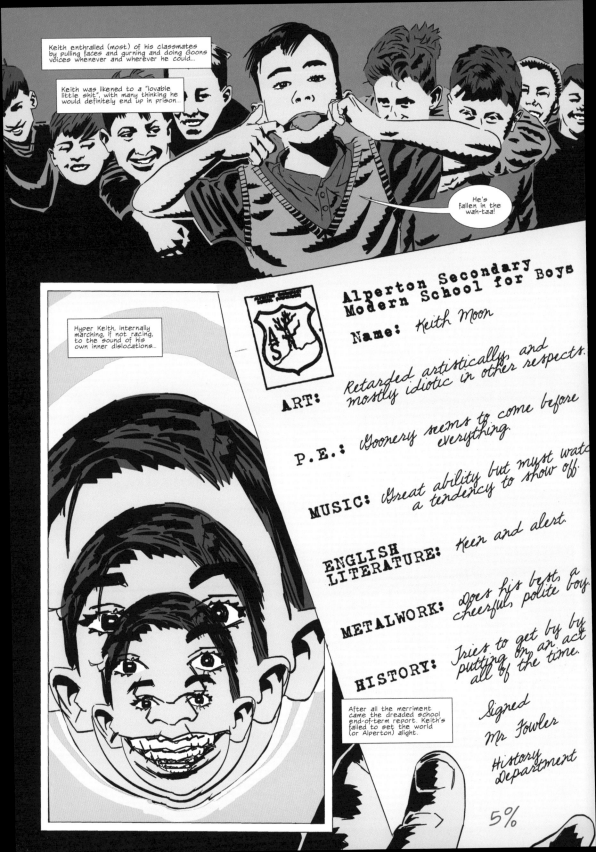

Keith was calling himself a "mental drummer", with no sense of incipient irony whatsoever...

In my mind,
I was becoming a drummer...
I was *already* a drummer --
a *mental* drummer. I gotta make
the reality connect to
my inner longings...

Oh look, here
comes Mr Sladden,
the geography teacher.
He can't catch me smoking
fags or he'll have my guts for
garters -- he'll have it back
to the headmaster and
then to my parents...

At 134 Chaplin Road, Keith took his pranksterism to new and novel heights... well, from bedroom window height anyway!

WHOOOOOOO WHOOOOOO
WHOOOOOOO
WHOOOOO

One way to wake up
the neighbourhood...

WHOOOOOO
WHOOOOOO

Keith's sense of mischief and his pranks got ever more inventive...

UUUUUrrrgggh! Bleeeuuurrfiirrrahhh! BLLLOOOOOOoz AAAARGGGGAHHHh!!

Gerry took a trip out to Chaplin Road and visited the Moons' residence...

A feast was laid on for Keith's guest -- just not in a way he had encountered before...

Keith managed to attend rehearsals for the new band that Gerry had joined, The Escorts.

The Prince Of Wales boozer on the Kingsbury Roundabout. These Escorts rehearsals occurred on a Sunday morning...

'Ere, Keith, if you can get the money together mate, you could buy that pearl blue kit in the store for 75 pounds. My boss says if you can sort it out, you can get it over a two year period on HP. Not bad, eh?

Keith managed to get that pearl blue kit back to his home. Alf, are you ready for the noise to come...?

Keith was becoming fixated by Carlo Little, the in-demand drummer doing the London gig circuits...

Everyone loved Carlo's drumming, he was considered a master of the new UK beat-style drums. He was killing everybody in Lord Sutch And The Savages...

Carlo
The
SAVAGES

I bin watching Carlo and The Savages with that new member on keyboards, Nicky Hopkins, and my old schoolmate Bernie Watson. This is what I want to do! I'm going to get around and go and see all the bands and really learn about music.

Keith's pranks took on a darker hue...

This is the Gestapo here! Please get in line for the gassings, please! Form a nice orderly queue at once!

Keith was now 16 years old and getting bored of The Escorts' limited musical ambitions and horizons. He was looking for newer, bigger opportunities...

Dad, can you drive me to an audition wiv this band called The Beachcombers?

You're too young, Keith. Come back in a year, mate!

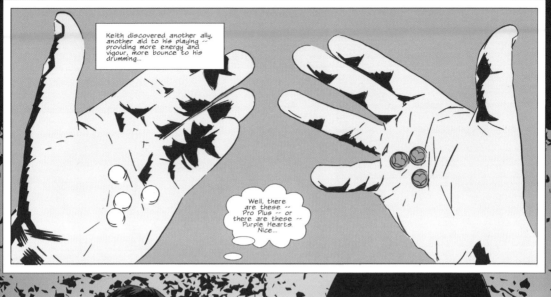

Fuck me! He's done more damage in a few minutes than I've ever done. Right flash, mad little bastard...

...I'm going to need a fiver on top of my session fee for all this damage.

Whatcha doing on Saturday?

Nothing, why?

We've got a gig -- you can do it if you want. We can pick you up in our van.

The Trade Union Hall, Watford.
The band is now billed as The Who.

That drummer is really great, he's holding all this dysfunctional energy together. Kit is right about these guys, they really have got something.

Meaden's single is a fucking disaster. We can't give the bastard away! And Helmut Gorden is about as managerial as my granny.

After seeing them at The Railway, I knew they could be bona fide superstars.

Lambert is a definite toff and he seems unstable, but he and Chris Stamp have a much-needed plan...

He came from an eccentric and very effusive family. His grandfather was an Australian painter and his father, Constant, a feted and famous composer...

Like Brian with The Beatles and Loog Oldham with The Stones, the 1960s offered a merging of the upper-middle classes and toffs with the working class bands on the rise...

'OK Kit, we've tried out the champers, it's your turn to try these. A few of these leapers will get you in the right frame of mind...

Talking of leapers, Pete Meaden was up and down like Tower Bridge. It was time for a parting of the ways.

Dearest Peter -- here is a non-refundable cheque as a token of our appreciation for your efforts to date. But things have to change -- as of now really, old boy...

£150.

Helmut Gorden got them on a bill with three-time Number One chart toppers Gerry And The Pacemakers -- but Gorden was swiftly jettisoned too...

Better than being called The Mars Bars, eh? Hehehehe...

ARE YOU LIKING IT TOOOOOOOO...

The High Numbers became The Who and Keith Moon firmed up their identity no end. He was the missing link -- the final and inescapable part of the chemistry puzzle...

...the totemic bassist...

...the roiling, disturbing tidal wave of guitar sound...

...with a sullen, charismatic front man...

...all allied to an enveloping hyper-energy driving all before it.

Lambert is a definite toff and he seems unstable...

The lighting rig bathes the band in deep red hues and heightens the effect of the onstage drama...

The scene was evolving fast and certain bands were stepping up to claim the crown...

YOU REEEAAALLY GOT ME...

On the circuit with all the biggest up-and-coming UK acts -- some amazing, like the diminutive Scottish raw soul-tinged singer Lulu...

...and some not to Keith's liking, like a singer called Val McCullam...

I hate this fucker's voice. Why are we backing up this prat? I couldn't give a thruppenny fuck....

Kit Lambert shot our first "movie" -- it was a short piece, four minutes' worth of celluloid and shot at The Scene...

It is one of the first and few films to capture the early mod scene...

Lambert and Stamp are trying to locate suitable areas in which to fully expedite the band...

Labels were passing on the band, first EMI on October 22, then Pye and just awhile later Fontana passed on a second single release...

We got to share a stage with these guys at the Blackpool Opera House...

THE BEATLES

At the Ivor Court Offices. Instead of being scattered all over London, we needed a sorted home base...

MARQUEE

November 24, 1964. The legendary and esteemed Marquee Club, London.

We broke the box office records that year and into 1965...

THE WHO

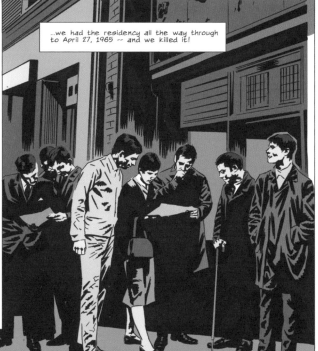

...we had the residency all the way through to April 27, 1965 -- and we killed it!

Shel Talmy had another breakthrough that came on some earlier demos... The band and Talmy's paths were to cross...

I CAN'T EXPLAIN... THINK IT'S LOVE...

This is the most gritty-sounding rock and roll in all of England... I'll get producer's royalties and points on these releases too. I fucked myself good and proper on the deal with The Kinks...

Pye Studios, London, late 1964...

TRY TO SAY IT TO YOU... WHEN I FEEL BLUE...

She had all the strictures of a Roman Catholic upbringing.

I didn't sleep around -- I was a good Catholic girl...

Keith's nice, I have spoken to him and he's very funny but he's not really what I'm looking for...

Bournemouth, on the southern coast of England, with its genteel gulf stream and discreet palm trees.

January 29, 1965. Ready Steady Go! was the show...

Kit Lambert was rumoured to have crowded the TV studio with the "100 faces" to make them look more popular... We'll never know...

Keith pursued Kim with ardour and infatuation, soon deepened into that mysterious state called love...

Another young mod called Rod Stewart liked Kim too -- and wanted to get to know her more...

The green-eyed monster would rise up...

You're talking to that big-nosed cunt Rod Stewart. He's a fucking bastard -- I wouldn't trust that fucker as far as I could throw him...

Within the band the usual rivalries began to grow and fester, beginning to bubble to the surface, barely repressed...

This Moon bastard is really starting to do my crust in. He's dead close to getting clocked, good and proper...

Style...
space...
attitude...

...we were on the verge of becoming a full-on volatile musical force... Anyway, Anyhow, Anywhere...

The looning about began in earnest...

Do you mind if I join you? I mean, join you...?

We've already got a drummer thanks you cheeky sod...

We did Ready Steady Go! 10 times in 1965...

READY STEADY GO

This was something that was to become a regular event over the years ahead.

This was how Richard Cole was to get to know Keith Moon. Little did anyone know....

An immediate downgrade to another, lesser hotel was in short order...

We were to sign with the independently launched record label Reaction, put together by the entrepreneurial Australian Robert Stigwood...

The deal our management, New Action, had signed with producer Shel Talmy was creatively brilliant and financially a total disaster...

Stigwood's Reaction record label was an unprecedented move in the cloistered, miserly UK record business at that time -- an independent taking on the tired old major labels at their own game.

Reaction was to be our new label in the UK. Kit Lambert took the single 'Substitute' to his pal Stigwood and the nascent label became our new home. In the USA, Atco handled the new single release...

I feel like I'm losing my mind -- everyone's suing everyone else. I thought we were supposed to be a band on the up, making great music, making it big...

Keith was just 20 years old and his drinking was increasing at an alarming rate...

The effects on Keith of the booze, the speed and other pills like Mandies and other downers were starting to tell...

They're talking about me in front of me and behind my back. I can't even remember playing on 'Substitute'... What's happening to my nut...?

Another behaviour was about to begin -- one that was destined to excite and ignite the crowds...

C'mon, Phil, lend me the left-hand side of your double bass drum kit -- I promise I won't wreck it, honest mate.

As the symbolic year 1967 approached, The Who upped their game and Pete Townshend wrote a mini-epic which foreshadowed later, even more ambitious works...

Her man's been gone for high on a year, he was due home yesterday...

In The Who camp things were fraught and claustrophobic as usual, and things were cramped at Chaplin Road. It was time for a house move...

The album had a jaunty single and a closing nine minutes of mini-operatics...

A film for the single 'Happy Jack' was shot at New Action's Mayfair offices...

The International Pop Festival was to be held in Monterey from June 16 through to 18, 1967...

The Beach Boys were to headline and close the festival Sunday night, but they withdrew. Maybe they were worried about all the heavy hitters on the bill...?

Their feet touched down on American soil once again...

The band needed to slot another prestigious West Coast gig in before Monterey. The Fillmore West... We played with some funky cats called Loading Zone, and we heard a new band on the up called Santana got canned by Bill Graham...

THE WHO
A Quick One

The International Pop Festival, Monterey.

Did Hendrix really just call me a honky? I told him about copying our act, to leave it out -- smashing up the guitars and all that stuff...

We opened the Monterey Festival on the Sunday evening. We went over alright but the stoned-out hippies really didn't seem to notice...

We made sure mayhem was produced. The Yanks had never seen anything like it...

Jimi Hendrix set his guitar on fire -- he totally ignored Pete Townshend's talking-to and set about smashing his guitar into his amps. The Who were well and truly upstaged...

Cherry bombs came in handy too when you wanted to wake people up, regardless of the hour of day...

In Birmingham, Alabama, Keith was refining ways to obliterate certain objects. Suitcases had a certain combustible quality...

BOOOOOOM!!

I am sooooo used to plain ol' English bangers -- these cherry bombs are great!

KRABBBOOOOM!

On August 23, 1967, Keith turned 21 in Flint, Michigan. A party was held in his honour in the Holiday Inn hotel. Things were to get plenty rowdy...

Keith eschewed pants and was caught with his trousers down or torn to shreds -- all in all, a heady 21st party. The no-pants look was essential for his extracurricular mooning antics...

Word of mouth escalated as things got noisier, and the cops were called to investigate what all the fuss was about...

There was damage everywhere -- the banqueting room, the swimming pool, cars covered in foam, walls and carpets ruined... The financials to cover all this came to an estimated $24,000 by some accounts...

It's dangerous to believe your own hype -- remember that for the future...

By the way -- the legendary story of me driving a car into the swimming pool: how do I top a tale that never even happened...?

The Who literally wrecked the stage at The Convention Center in Asbury Park in New Jersey. Everybody got pissed at Keith's playing. Was it the downers? Keith decided to leave the band, yet again and in a very dramatic style...

Love letters straight to your heart...

Keith and Kim had to leave Ormonde Terrace and moved again to a flat above Pearl's Garages in Highgate...

Roger Daltrey was honing his stagecraft and this suited a monumental song that Pete Townshend had just created. This new brooding song was recorded in New York, Nashville and Los Angeles... It needed a long leash as it was a surge of barely controlled aggression and menace...

Pop became "rock" -- that year Sgt Pepper's changed the playing field overnight and forever...

WOKE UP ONE MORNING HALF ASLEEP...

CAROLINE

All this was swelled by the invaluable airplay by the pirate radio stations like Radio Caroline... but after the government ban outlawing the stations, Radio 1 was invented to grab some of the new, lucrative rock action. People were smelling big money... Radio 1 kicked off with 'Flowers In The Rain' by The Move on September 30, 1967.

As for The Move, they tried to ape our act under their manager, the hustling Tony Secunda: the auto-destruction, the aggressive, surly stage show -- and they could play. For a bit we thought they were real contenders. People said they could give us a run for our money...

...YOU BETTER WATCH YOUR STEP...

The Who recorded a commercial for Coca-Cola and this gave rise to the ironically titled The Who Sell Out. Keith and John, in between drinks, composed part of the mini-commercial breaks on the album...

The new album
arrived in early
1968. For some
reason 'I Can
See For Miles'
did not sell as
well as
expected...

...maybe its
glowering
aural menace
did not fit
the beatific
vibe of that
year...

...but in the USA,
'I Can See For Miles'
became a Top 10 hit...

I KNOW YOU'VE DECEIVED ME, NOW HERE'S A SURPRISE...

In London, the
ever-inventive
Keith found a
new way to play
the drums...

Management seemed to rarely personally manage -- perhaps mismanage -- and certainly allowed the untrammelled wildness to take free reign...

The management themselves were taking the high road literally to the outer edges of excess...

...as was Keith.

Over on 55th Street at The Gorham Hotel, and on the very same fated day that Martin Luther King was assassinated...

...on the ninth floor, Keith found a new skewed direction. The other members of The Who were less enthusiastic...

Frank Barsalona had his work cut out here...

C'mon, Keith, come on back in... We'll tell the cops you're on some strong medication here and you've had a real bad reaction...

The toilet in his hotel room was also totalled before his excursion out onto the ledge...

...There will damages to be paid here to the hotel, and the management don't want you back -- ever!

A prestigious photo session for LIFE magazine was almost nixed due to Keith getting narked. The band were really pissed off with him but it all went ahead...

Word got back to Kim -- Keith's ardour was being spread away from home. Alison Entwistle, while on the US tour, saw some eye-opening sights. She felt protective of Kim...

Kim, there's something you ought to know...

A pet fox kept the kids alright -- well, for a while at least...

The champagne bottle embedded in the lounge wall was a reminder of Keith and Kim's rows.

The management moved offices, over to Old Compton Street in Soho to be precise. Keith loved being back there and thought nothing of inviting laggards back to the Highgate flat after nights out at The Speakeasy...

Long-suffering Kim got the kettle on for the various stragglers...

BEEEP! BEEEP! BEEEEEEEPF

In 1968, both 'Dogs' and the 'Magic Bus' single, with its hip Bo Diddley clave beat, died a death, sales-wise...

John and Keith felt The Who had reached the end of their line. They were seeing a new happening band forming and thought of joining. They even thought up a name -- Lead Zeppelin...

In Newcastle, Keith had time to engage in further visual diversions.

Ooooh, oooooohhhh... Help! Help! I am being molested!

The Tommy writing process was in gestation, adding 'Pinball Wizard' and 'Tommy's Holiday Camp' to alleviate some of the perceived "spiritual piety" of Pete Townshend's lyrics...

It eventually evolved into a concept album a la Sgt Peppers, Ogdens' Nut Gone Flake, SF Sorrow and more...

'Pinball Wizard' was released in March and went to Number Four in the UK without any trouble...

The Tommy suite was presented in its entirety at Ronnie Scott's Jazz Club in Soho, London that May.

ronnie scott's CLUB
JAZZ NIGHTLY

Keith's wall of sound, a kind of kinetic aural explosion, was unheard of before, and also entirely untaught. It was something that couldn't be taught -- it's like trying to describe a car crash that somehow always resolves in space and time...

You have to know the rules to break them. Keith didn't know the rules but he still broke them...

What's Keith doing? It's amazing but I can't work it out for the life of me...

The band did The Royal Albert Hall with Chuck Berry...

...Tommy went through the roof, an instant Top Five hit on both sides of the water -- a hit out of the box, and 'Pinball Wizard' followed in its wake too.

What's all this about a blind kid in your song, Pete?

We were hot again everywhere -- we played to 40,000 at The National Jazz And Blues Festival, then over to Massachusetts to play in front of 20,000, and then...

...there was Woodstock... We got a $13,000 fee but the band hated it. The idiotic hippies slipped us acid before we went on live -- so we were tripping and going on 16 hours late onstage...

Pete Townshend was beyond enraged... He booted the upstart Abbie Hoffman up the arse and off the stage when he tried to invade the stage during the band's fiery performance...

Fuck off, fuck off my fucking stage!!

Neil Boland was taken to Queen Elizabeth The Second hospital but was dead on arrival...

We performed Tommy in its entirety at The New York Metropolitan Opera House. Back home, Keith had Kim overseeing the pub he had invested in called The Crown And Cushion in Chipping Norton..

The Isle Of Wight Festival, August 26 to 31, 1970, with The Who appearing on Saturday 29.

The brio and optimism of the 1960s were heading full tilt towards oblivion. Jimi Hendrix choked on his own vomit in London, with Janis Joplin following him to an early grave two weeks later. They'd all gone and joined the 27 club...

Jim Morrison of The Doors was also to join this spectral list. Imagine The Doors having to precede The Who at The Isle Of Wight Festival -- a thankless task...

All this guff is spoken about the Sixties... I think rock 'n' rollers just changed the length of their hair and very little else.

Keith started to dress up -- he assumed other egos, other personal miens...

I love dressing up -- it's something I have to do. Don't ask me why though... I don't know what makes me want to do it...

Sometimes the dressing up could become a little... "out there", shall we say...? The Nazi uniforms came out of their respective wardrobes for some serious carousing -- much to the chagrin of certain onlookers...

...and with Viv Stanshall as willing accomplice and close friend the ante was upped immediately...

Keith had already been thrown out bodily from the German Bierkeller in London's Bond Street and now he and Viv Stanshall were taking it a stage further -- throwing Nazi shapes in an open-top Mercedes whilst driving through the Jewish area of Golders Green...

Sieg heil! Sieg heil!

Donner und Blitzen... swinehunts!

It appeared that Keith was taking the self-destruction further and further. Kim left with Mandy after yet another major row. All were openly wounded, words were said, apologies made -- nothing changed...

Was Kim coming back home...? Unsure and in fearful dread, Keith moved back to Chelsea. He involved himself in more dressing up for Frank Zappa's film folly 200 Motels...

Sleep is for wankers, I'm staying up for the duration...

The Zappa movie, although a chaotic mess on release, gave Pete Townshend the further impetus to become a movie developer. That initial project became Lifehouse. That never lit up any cinema screens but a new Who album was to emerge from this aborted project...

WHO'S NEXT

Lifehouse was aborted because the concept was too far out for anyone but Pete to understand, but the songs he'd written became Who's Next, co-produced by Glyn Johns, a towering achievement...

Keith played to a click track and the drumming was reined into stricter tempos, giving the music form. Glyn Johns attempted to nail down heavier beats and keep Keith's wayward fills to a manageable amount...

A finely balanced production was allied to kicking ensemble playing...

Where is Kim...? I can't stand it when she's not back at home. I've heard she's staying in Ealing somewhere...

Keith found Kim's bolthole in Ealing and begged her forgiveness in a rather direct manner, very late at night...

Keith and Kim resolved their differences and moved in together again. This time Keith had bought a bizarre house called Tara in Chertsey. Tara was a cuboid and pyramid-shaped folly. It had a handy pub called The Golden Grove at the end of the drive...

Keith was just 25 and heading towards becoming a millionaire...

Juliet! Kim! Kim! What light from yonder window breaks... It is the East and Kim is the sun...

Keith and Kim enjoyed some carefree days, some golden halcyon days. Could they ever end...? Everyone hoped not... The legend grew, the stories of King Keith in his castle at Tara...

...Keith lavishly bestowed upon his nearest and dearest, befitting his ascending fame and rock royalty...

Who's Next charted at Number One in the UK and Top Five in the USA. 'Won't Get Fooled Again' was a bona fide instant rock anthem...

A new minder was called in to look after Keith in his many wayward moments. He was Doug Butler and for six years Doug was Keith's minder, fixer and right-hand man. The Golden Goose became a home from home...

Fast cars were bought, sold or discarded. 1972 saw the money pile in, but it was spent with an amazing alacrity...

The booze consumption continued apace -- two bottles of brandy and two bottles of champagne a day at least -- and these being mixed together. The drinking was starting earlier -- in fact, first thing in the morning...

The ability to have "one drink" was a thing of the past. It was all or nothing and the thought of abstinence was the furthest thing from Keith's mind at this stage of the game. All the same, Keith had been checked into a Weybridge clinic to "dry out"...

After leaving detox in Weybridge, Keith got a good part in That'll Be The Day, a hotly tipped film with teen star David Essex and Keith's running pal Ringo Starr in leading roles. It was both an acting and filmic success...

Buoyed by his acting debut, Keith took on the role of Uncle Ernie in the Tommy performance with The London Symphony Orchestra at London's Rainbow Theatre. Tommy wouldn't go away -- it kept selling and selling.

Boozers were drawn like flies to the bottle. Just about anyone was welcome to join in Keith's drunken ongoing binges...

...the feeling was that Keith was changing drastically out at Tara. He was entering another orbit -- a dangerous one...

His stomach was pumped to avoid total alcohol seizures. Keith also had a near-death spasm after ingesting heroin at Mountain guitarist Leslie West's house in London...

It was a definate form of self-administered Russian Roulette -- with more than one bullet in the gun -- at all times..

The decadence became more unbridled as the idealistic 1960s gave way to the intemperate, ego-driven and drug-addled 1970s. Keith was becoming more and more hollowed out...

I HAVE NO REAL SELF-DOUBTS
REAL SELF-WORTH HELP!
DOES KIM REALLY LOVE ME...? AM I ANY GOOD
IS MY PLAYING THAT GOOD...?
DOES PETE REALLY LIKE ME, OR ANY OF THE OTHER GUYS...?

He feels life so intensely, so deeply. People need him to be crazy all the time... but it's becoming more frightening to keep this game up...

I'm scared, I'm everybody's clown... Everything is really sour between me and Kim...

His young daughter, Mandy, was totally confused throughout all the madness being enacted. She was shown a picture of Adolf Hitler and she thought it was her dad.

The band began work on what was to become Quadrophenia. By then, Roger Daltrey had started looking at the band's finances and there was a huge black hole -- all the drugs, booze and assorted madness was sucking out the cash. Bill Curbishley was called in to oversee the band's parlous finances and day-to-day band management...

The cracks in the management relationship with Lambert and Stamp became critical. A cheque advance from Kit Lambert bounced and then the game was up...

Quadrophenia was another of Pete's grand concepts, seen as a bit over the top, but time has cast a much kinder glow over the story of Jimmy and the emerging mod generation...

BELL BOY! I GOT TO KEEP RUNNING NOW. BELL BOY! KEEP MY LIP BUTTONED DOWN...

Keith sang the song 'Bell Boy' and emphasised the growing self-awareness of the main character Jimmy as the story of Quadrophenia came into its final act.

A film of Tommy was to be helmed by controversial director Ken Russell, with Keith reprising his role as Uncle Ernie. It seemed there was so much to look forward to...

...but Kim had had enough. She was leaving Keith and Tara. Perhaps in her heart she had already left...

Kim, Kim! You've got to come with me, you've got to come back to Tara!

The two kids, Dermott, Kim's younger brother, and Mandy were unceremoniously hustled into a taxi next day and sent to Kim, who was staying at The Runnymede Hotel...

...Kim, after hastily picking up some further possessions, never set foot in Tara again.

The routines of stomach pumping and overnight hospital admissions continued...

The inner anguish and loneliness are unbearable. I'm getting more of the medicine I crave but I'm not feeling anything at all... and there's no Kim, no Dermott, no Mandy...

...and then all of a sudden, no Alf. Keith's dad had a heart attack on the way to hospital. He was just 53.

Ollie Reed and Keith Moon were destined to be friends -- united by a ferocious thirst and a need for combined artistic insanity...

Keith showed me the way from the bar to the bizarre... He showed me the way to total insanity...

Keith started "blacking out". He was drinking with no memories of what he had been doing -- or even while he was doing it.

That'll Be The Day did very well and a sequel was planned. Stardust was the result, again with David Essex in the lead role. Keith failed his audition for a larger acting part, or at least his eyebrows did... Keith essentially was becoming a pest. It was going from social boozing to destructive hard drinking...

Keith flew out to Los Angeles and immediately linked up with the extant expat party animals. Ringo Starr and John Lennon were there, and Harry Nilsson and Jesse Ed Davis tagged along to balance out the transatlantic troubadour lunacy...

All these men were still riding high -- very high -- but underneath the surface things were askance.

DOOOON'T WOOOOORREEE BABEEE...

Mal Evans, who had been The Beatles' road manager, was chosen by Keith to produce a favourite song in the studio...

The Tommy soundtrack was being recorded mostly without Keith and with none of his magic playing. Director Ken Russell moved the time period and shifted the emphasis filmically from Keith's Uncle Ernie to Ollie Reed's Uncle Frank.

DOWN WITH THE BEDCLOTHES, UP WITH THE NIGHTSHIRT! FIDDLE ABOUT, FIDDLE ABOUT, FIDDLE ABOUT!

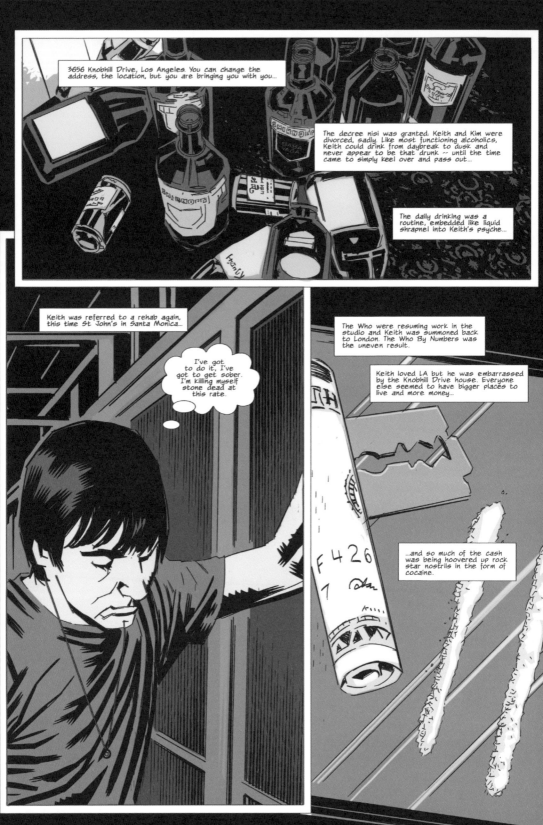

The touring began again: money was needed and a whole 12 months of work lay ahead. Keith also had very pressing matters to attend to. He attended initial therapy sessions with the feted Dr Meg Patterson, who had helped Eric Clapton with his severe addiction issues...

I have never said this before to a client -- well, especially at our first session -- but, you don't need my treatment, you need Jesus Christ!

I absolutely agree with you, but how do I find Him?

I believe all this hinges on your search for happiness and fame. With all the drugs and drink, you have been and are opening a door to the occult. I believe your real problem is a deep spiritual one. These things can invade us when we leave our "doors" open, so to speak, through the use of alcohol and drugs...

By selling your soul for more and more -- more of what the world has to offer -- power, money, fame, sex -- and just more, more, more -- I believe you are being totally controlled by your fears, Keith. This is a deep, spiritual fear.

Keith wanted Meg Patterson to go on tour with The Who -- to examine his spiritual occultic "familiars" as he described them...

Was Keith, with his split personality, an incipient schizophrenic...?

With Meg's guidance, Keith appeared to stay straight for a while. This was a real first! But it didn't last long...

...he collapsed again, onstage at Boston.

Bill Curbishley, The Who's new manager, was beside himself -- getting to his own brink of rage against Keith, who had just badly injured himself in yet another drunken blackout.

356

Trancas in Los Angeles, a new, beautiful split-level seafront home for Keith, more befitting his rock star status.

With punk beating down the door of the established rock 'n' roll hierarchy over the pond in the UK, Keith was feeling even more isolated and fragile, if that were possible...

...even his neighbour in the next beachfront house along, famous film star Steve McQueen, didn't want to know him...

Self-destruction at full tilt on a daily basis, but deep in his eyes was an overwhelming fear. It was impossible to keep it at bay...

Keith returned to the UK. Being on the beach at Trancas was a disaster. He was lonely, bored and often broke...

I can't drum without booze. Give me that fucking brandy and then I can play -- I think... I am in denial... I'm in denial about the drink...

WHO ARE YOU... OOO OOO, OOO OOO...

In the studio, recording the album Who Are You, Keith rallied again...

I will have a holiday with Annette, I'll make it up to Mandy and Dermott -- everything will be alright...

After a relatively idyllic break, Keith returned with Annette to Nilsson's flat in Curzon Place, London...

Everything's going to be alright now. Dr Diamond has put me on a course of Heminevrin to help me deal with the booze withdrawals... I'm going to stop this time -- for good.

Keith did stop, and this time for good.

Could Keith have made it? The chances are less than average, with just a small percentage of alcoholics and addicts maintaining abstinence and living addiction-free lives.

Was Keith at the stage where he wanted to want to stop? We'll never know...

The man takes a drink...
then the drink takes a drink...
then the drink takes the man...

The alcoholic is defiant to the last. The ego-shattering
needed to puncture the wall of this illusion is difficult.
Who really cares to admit complete defeat?

Alcohol is the great leveller. This is a bankruptcy
that nothing or no one can withstand -- neither
money, sex, power or success.

Keith may have had a fatal accident --
the pills mixed disastrously with the booze...

...but so few make it, the toll is
immense. It's a sobering thought.

You were loved, Keith, even if you
didn't know it or feel it. You really
were... loved...

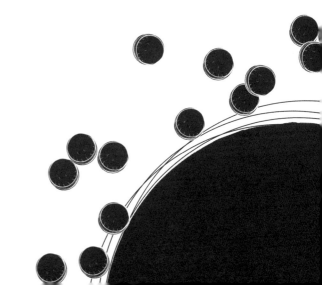

DRAWING A YOUNG KEITH

A CHALLENGE! WITH VERY LITTLE REFERENCE MATERIAL AVAILABLE, I HAD TO IMPROVISE. IT WAS A MATTER OF DRAWING FROM A REFERENCE OF HIM AS AN ADULT AND CUTTING AWAY AT THE JAWLINE. THEN, IF HE'LL PARDON ME, I GAVE HIM A SLIGHT NOSE JOB, TO PROVIDE THE YOUNG KEITH WITH THAT 'BABY FACE.'

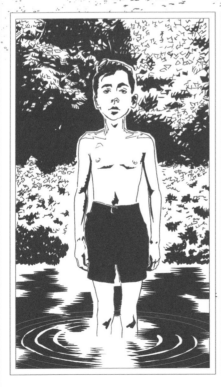

DRAWING DRUMKITS

AT THE RISK OF SOUNDING LIKE SOME SORT OF A SADIST, I ACTUALLY ENJOYED DRAWING THEM (HANDY FOR A COMIC ABOUT THE WORLD'S MOST ICONIC DRUMMER). I FOUND THAT THE LESS I WORRIED ABOUT THE SMALL, MECHANICAL DETAIL, THE BETTER THE RESULT. I THINK THAT WE DON'T REALLY SEE THE WORLD IN GREAT DETAIL, WE'RE TOO BUSY, SO THAT'S HOW I DREW IT.

WHO ARE YOU? GALLERY

A PAGE I ENJOY

I LIKE THE SIMPLICITY HERE, HOW
EVERYTHING SEEMS TO BE ENVELOPED BY
THE BLACKS AND IS GIVEN WEIGHT BY IT.
AGAIN, IT'S ABOUT HAVING ENOUGH DETAIL,
BUT NOT SO MUCH AS TO MAKE THE EYE
DWELL ON IT. THE READER NEEDS TO SKIP
EASILY FROM ONE PANEL TO THE NEXT...
AND I GOT TO DRAW JIMI HENDRIX!!

IMPACT AND EMPHASIS!

SO JIM ASKED FOR AN EXPLOSION IN KEITH'S HEAD ON THIS PAGE. OBVIOUSLY THAT'S NOT SOMETHING THAT COULD BE SQUIRRELED AWAY INTO THE CORNER. SO HERE, BECAUSE WE'VE GOT A FAIRLY IMPORTANT SECONDARY PANEL (THE APPEARANCE OF THE LEGENDARY CHUCK BERRY!), IT WAS A MATTER OF TRYING TO AFFORD EVERYTHING THE RIGHT AMOUNT OF EMPHASIS... OVER THREE, NON-SEQUENTIAL PANELS... AND LEAVING ENOUGH ROOM FOR LETTERING... DO YOU FEEL SORRY FOR ME YET?

JIM McCARTHY

Jim McCarthy's career in publishing began with *2000AD* and work on *Bad Company*, *Bix Barton*, *The Grudgefather*, *Kyd Cyborg* and *Judge Dredd*.

He has also immersed himself in American music forms and culture, resulting in *Voices Of Latin Rock*, which was published by Hal Leonard. It is the first book to examine Santana, Latin rock culture and the Mission District, the area where this nascent political and musical art form emerged. This is one of the radical birth points of Hispanic music, art and culture.

Voices Of Latin Rock led to a series of concerts in San Francisco promoting autism awareness and which featured Carlos Santana, Booker T, Los Lobos, Sly Stone, George Clinton, El Chicano, Malo, Taj Mahal and The Doobie Brothers, among others.

Jim is also engaged in producing insightful, contemporary graphic novels, linked to music subjects. The most recent was *Living for Kicks: A Mods Graphic Novel*. Other graphic biographies have covered Metallica, The Ramones, The Sex Pistols, Kurt Cobain, Michael Jackson, Tupac Shakur, Eminem and Bob Marley.

"You can do whatever you want within a graphic novel. You can be very cinematic and put things in that you couldn't in a traditional biography, and maybe not even in a film. You can come at it from different angles, different tenses, different points of view. You can use visual symbols to make a lot of comments in a single panel. When it comes to televised music documentaries, they seem to follow a prescribed path. I try to approach each one in a different way."

Jim McCarthy

www.jimmccarthy.co.uk

MARC OLIVENT

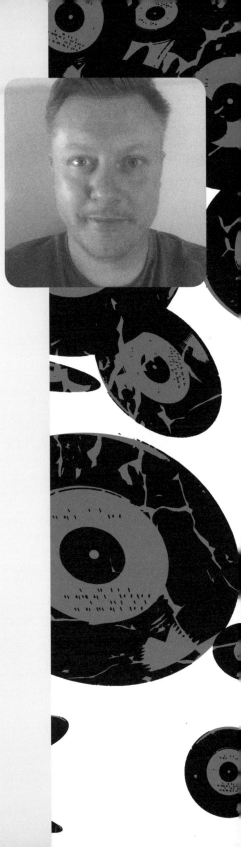

Marc Olivent is a freelance illustrator based in Lincoln. He specialises in comic book illustration, a passion he developed at a very early age by reading (and re-reading and re-reading...) Seventies and Eighties Stan Lee-created Marvel comics. From those early days, Marc knew exactly where his career path lay (although it took a little longer to get there than he first envisaged).

He never stopped reading comics and would study the visual storytelling techniques employed by the masters of the craft. His influences are many, but his style is all his own (be that a good or bad thing!).

Previous work includes Dark Horse Presents strip 'Sundown Crossroads', 'Rick Fury' and 'Zezi' for ROK Comics and *Dark Satanic Mills* for Walker Books, on which he worked with legendary comics illustrator John Higgins (*Watchmen*, *Judge Dredd*). *Dark Satanic Mills* was nominated for the 2015 Kate Greenaway award for illustration.

This is his second book for Omnibus Press, following *Reckless Life: Guns N' Roses — A Graphic Novel*.

www.marcolivent.wix.com

LIVING FOR KICKS

a mods graphic novel

Jim McCarthy & Kevin Cross

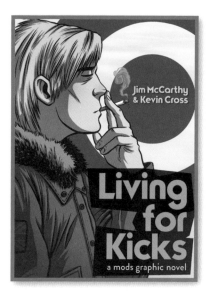

Living for Kicks is an electrifying graphic novel that brings the British pop culture of the 1960s to vivid life.

It focusses on Spike Spellane, a young Mod trying to hustle enough money to start a record label in London's sleazy Soho. His adventures are skilfully interwoven with the antics of real-life heroes and villains while the settings are contemporary locations that made the headlines and helped shape a tumultuous decade.

Spellane's story embraces legendary Soho jazz dives, famous gangsters and real music stars. It takes place against the background of the notorious Christine Keeler scandal that rocked the country and almost brought down a government. Real life also provided the setting for the novel's spectacular climax – the infamous battles between Mods and Rockers staged on the beaches of southern England.

Living for Kicks shows and tells exactly what it was like to be a mover and shaker during a unique era of British pop creativity and social upheaval.

Available from all good bookshops
Or in case of difficulty **www.omnibuspress.com**

Order No: OP55902
ISBN: 978.1.78305.578.4